CONTENTS

Introduction   3

Soup   7

Fish   11

Meat   15

Puddings   30

Cakes   41

Bread and Scones   51

Savoury Dishes and Drinks   57

METRIC CONVERSION TABLES

Solids

An exact conversion from imperial to metric measurements is totally impractical for cooking purposes, the equivalent of 1 ounce being 28.35 grams. The following table provides a satisfactory basis for converting recipes; although the metric equivalents are about 10% above the imperial measurements, the proportions are retained.

OUNCES	GRAMS	OUNCES	GRAMS
1	30	9	280
2	60	10	315
3	90	11	345
4	125	12	375
5	155	13	410
6	185	14	440
7	220	15	470
8	250	16	500

Liquids and Cup Measures

The 8-fluid ounce (227 ml.) measuring cup will be replaced by a standard 250-millilitre metric measuring cup. The comparative imperial and metric graduations are set out below:

IMPERIAL		METRIC	
fl. oz.	cup	cup	ml.
1			30
2	$\frac{1}{4}$	$\frac{1}{4}$	
	$\frac{1}{3}$	$\frac{1}{3}$	
3			100
4	$\frac{1}{2}$	$\frac{1}{2}$	
5 ($\frac{1}{4}$ pt.)			
6	$\frac{3}{4}$	$\frac{3}{4}$	
8	1	1	250

The metric teaspoon is 5 ml., and the tablespoon 20 ml. (15 ml. in New Zealand); the imperial ones are equivalent to 3.6 ml. and 14.2 ml. respectively.

INTRODUCTION

'I will venture to affirm that cookery in England, when well done, is superior to that of any country in the world.'
Samuel Ude, 1833

When I was a little girl in Shropshire, in the English Midlands, in the 1950s, traditional English cookery still flourished throughout the English countryside. You could still easily buy farm fresh food, traditional cheeses, fruit straight from the orchard, butter that *was* butter, real fresh eggs, and vegetables direct from the garden.

I remember our big, cosy country kitchen, with sides of bacon hanging from the rafters. Life seemed to centre round the warm Aga stove. We would chat and gossip there, or toast ourselves before the coal fire nearby. My mother would bustle about making the roast beef and Yorkshire pudding, or shepherd's pie, or beefsteak and kidney pudding, one of my father's favourite dishes.

My mother encouraged us to help, and make things ourselves, so that we all learnt to love cooking — and eating the results — from an early age. We used to stand on chairs and stir pans on the stove, and make things from scraps of pastry. As we grew older, we tried our hands at cakes and various recipes passed down by our grandmothers. My grandmother would take hours mincing and chopping up the ingredients for faggots, and beautiful soups. How many children are given this chance now?

I remember a Yorkshire dales kitchen with its fire-warmed oven, stone flags, jars of home-made gooseberry jam, trays of turf cakes, and bottles of dandelion wine.

I remember a snug cottage kitchen in the Cumberland hills, rich with the smells of fresh gingerbread and plank bread straight from the oven, and glasses of delicious elder-flower wine.

I remember watching an old Shropshire lady cooking her joint of beef on a spit over a fire, so that the fat dripped down on to the Yorkshire pudding — and superb it was to eat.

I remember eating Singing Hinnies in Northumberland; Welsh lamb in Merionethshire; Cornish pasties in Penzance; clotted cream, strawberry jam, and scones in Devonshire; and real Cheddar cheese in Somerset.

English cookery has a great and varied tradition. Many of its old recipes and regional variations, its sauces and its cheeses, have sadly been lost. Since the last war at least, the English have been rather modest about or indifferent to their native cookery. The fashionable thing was to go in for the glamour of French cuisine or exotic Oriental or Mediterranean cooking. All this is very fine, of course, but many millions of good cooks would agree that for nourishment, comfort, richness, and dependability, traditional English cookery cannot be excelled. And their husbands would agree with them! For what can rival, at the end of a long, hard day, Lancashire hotpot, properly cooked? Or English crumpets, oozing with butter; or the vigour and taste bud sensation of regional English cheeses; or the sweetness and variety of English puddings and cakes?

The stodgy, heavy name that English cookery has in some quarters is often an indictment of the cook. Of course, the English climate calls for solid food — but there are exciting, lighter recipes to be found.

We live in an age of pre-cooked, packaged, and frozen foods, canned fruit, and TV dinners. They are convenient, of course, but they are dull and mediocre. Good and enterprising cooks everywhere can still summon up the glorious tastes and comfortable sensations that come from English cookery at its best.

It has a long history, its roots in the strong culture and regionalism of the lovely and fruitful English countryside.

I have personally used, often many times, every recipe in this book. Many of them I learnt from my family and relations and friends in the English country-side.

I hope this little guide will help its readers to put together some fine meals which they will, as the immortal Mrs Beeton says: 'Eat with good appetite'.

SOUP

Mutton Broth

1½ lb neck of lamb,
   hogget, or mutton
1 tbsp barley
salt and pepper
2-3 leeks, sliced

2 stalks of celery, sliced
1 small turnip, sliced
3 pt cold water
1½ tbsps chopped parsley

Remove fat from meat. Cut up as much meat as possible, from the bone. Wash the barley in a sieve; season well with salt and pepper. Place meat, bones, and vegetables in a saucepan with the water. Bring slowly to the boil and skim thoroughly. Add the barley and

simmer until the meat and vegetables are cooked —
about 2 to 3 hours. Remove the bones, add the chopped
parsley, and serve.

Oxtail Soup and Dumplings

Soup

1 oxtail	*2 oz bacon*
1 oz butter	*1 bouquet garni*
3 onions, chopped	*salt and pepper*
2 carrots, sliced	*3 tbsps flour*
2 sticks of celery, sliced	*chopped parsley*
4 pt stock	*(optional)*

Dumplings

4 oz self-raising flour	*salt and pepper*
2 oz suet	*water*

Soup: Ask the butcher to joint the oxtail. Carefully trim
all excess fat from the oxtail and fry it in the butter with
the prepared vegetables until brown. Cover with the
stock and bring to the boil, adding the chopped bacon,
bouquet garni, and salt and pepper to taste. Place lid on
the saucepan and simmer gently for 3½ hours. Skim the
fat off the soup, if necessary, as it cools. Strain the soup,
remove the meat from the bones, and cut it up. Return
the liquor and meat to the pan and reheat. Mix the flour
with a little water and add to the soup. Stir well until
the soup thickens. Add dumplings and cook for 15 to 20
minutes at simmering point. Serve sprinkled with
chopped parsley.
Dumplings: Mix the flour, suet, and seasoning together with enough water to make a dough. Divide it
into about eighteen small rounds.

Mulligatawny Soup

1 apple, peeled and
  chopped
2 onions, chopped
3 carrots, chopped
½ green pepper, chopped
8 oz tomatoes, peeled and
  finely chopped
2 sticks of celery,
  chopped
2 oz butter
1¾ pt stock, preferably
  brown
1½-2 tbsps curry powder

3 cloves
1 tbsp chopped parsley
sugar
salt and pepper
3 level tbsps cornflour
¼ pt milk
left-over cold meat or
  cooked chicken, cut
  into small cubes
1 oz cooked rice

Cook the apple and vegetables in the butter for 5 minutes. Add the stock, curry powder, cloves, parsley, sugar, and seasoning. Cover and simmer for 2 to 2½ hours. Sieve the soup and reheat. Blend the flour and milk until it forms a smooth cream. Stir in a small quantity of the hot soup and return the mixture to the pan. Drop in the chicken and rice and bring the soup to the boil, stirring until it thickens. Cook for another 2 to 3 minutes. Season again if necessary before serving.

Cream of Onion Soup

2 onions, sliced
1 oz margarine or butter
1 bouquet garni
1½ pt white stock

¼ pt milk
3 level tbsps flour
salt and pepper
3-4 tbsps cream

Lightly fry the onions in the butter for 6 minutes, until

soft but not coloured. Add the *bouquet garni* and stock, cover, bring to the boil, and simmer for about 50 minutes, until the onions are cooked. Blend or sieve the soup and reheat. Blend the milk and flour to a smooth cream, stir in a little of the hot soup, and return to pan. Season, bring to the boil, and stir until the soup thickens. Cook for a further 2 to 3 minutes. Stir the cream in just before serving the soup.

Leek Soup

1 bunch of leeks (about 6)
3 tbsps butter
3 large potatoes, sliced
1½ pt water and 2 chicken
   stock-cubes

salt and pepper
½ pt milk

Wash the leeks thoroughly and cut into 1-inch slices. Fry in the butter until soft; do not allow the leeks to become brown or crispy. Add the potatoes to the leeks, together with the chicken stock and seasoning. Simmer gently over a low heat until the vegetables are cooked. Add the milk and thoroughly heat, but do not allow to boil; then serve.

FISH

Trout and Almonds

4 small trout, about 4-6 oz
* each*
seasoned flour
6 oz butter

2 oz slivered blanched
* almonds*
juice of ½ lemon

Scale and clean the trout (rainbow trout are usually the best, but freshly caught brown trout are excellent), leaving the heads on. Wash and wipe them and coat them with the seasoned flour. Melt 4 ounces of the butter in a big frying pan. Fry the fish, two at a time, turning them once only, until they are tender and golden; this takes from 10 to 15 minutes. Drain the fish and keep them warm in a low oven or warming drawer. Clean the pan and melt remaining butter. Add the almonds and heat until lightly browned; add lemon juice and pour over fish.

Fish and Chips

Fish

1 - 1½ lb filleted cod,	*¼ pt water*
butterfish, or other	*salt and pepper*
suitable fish	*fat or oil*
4 oz flour	
1 egg	

Chips

2 lb potatoes	*fat or oil*

Fish: Combine the flour, egg, water, and seasoning to make a stiff cooking batter. Beat well until smooth. Coat the fish with the batter by dipping the fish into it. Heat the fat or oil to 350° to 375°F. and deep-fry for about 20 minutes in the normal way. Drain on paper towels or newspaper.

Chips: Peel the potatoes and cut into chips about ¼ to ½ inch in diameter. Dry well with a cloth. Heat the fat or oil to 350° to 375°F. A good way of finding the right cooking temperature is to drop a chip into the oil; if the chip rises to the top surrounded by bubbles, then the oil is hot enough. Quarter fill the pan with chips and cook for 6 to 7 minutes. Drain well. When all the chips are done, reheat the oil and fry the chips quickly for about 3 minutes until brown and crispy. Drain well.

Soused Herrings

8 fresh herrings
1 Spanish onion, sliced
1 dsp pickling spice
salt and pepper
1 bay-leaf
vinegar
water

Wash and scale the herrings, cut off their heads, and take out the backbones. Place a slice of onion in the middle of each fish. Beginning at the neck end of each herring, roll the fish up tightly, then place the herrings close together in a pie-dish. Sprinkle in the pickling spice and season to taste with salt and pepper. Add the bay-leaf. Pour in equal quantities of brown vinegar and water to come three-quarters of the way up the fish and bake the herrings in a moderate oven (350°F) for 40 minutes.

Haddock Soufflé

8 oz smoked haddock,
* cod, or other suitable*
* white fish*
2 level tbsps cornflour
½ pt milk
a knob of butter
3-4 oz grated cheese
1-2 eggs, separated
salt and pepper

Grease a 2-pint ovenproof dish. Put fish in a saucepan with enough water to cover, and bring to the boil. Allow to cool, then skin and flake it. Blend the cornflour with 2 tablespoons of the cold milk. Boil the rest of the milk with the butter; add to the blended cornflour, stirring well. Return mixture to pan and heat until boiling, stirring until the sauce thickens.

Take away from the heat. Add the cheese, fish, and egg-yolks and season well. Whisk the egg-whites stiffly and fold into the mixture. Pour into the dish and bake near the top of a hot oven (400°F) for about 20 minutes. The *soufflé* should be well risen and golden. Serve immediately: the mixture sinks as it cools.

Kedgeree
A traditional British breakfast

12 oz smoked haddock or salt
  smoked cod *cayenne pepper*
6 oz rice *parsley*
3 hard-boiled eggs
3 oz butter

Wash the fish, place in a saucepan of cold water, and bring slowly to the boil. Remove the pan from the stove and let it stand for 10 to 15 minutes. Drain off water. Skin the fish and flake it. Cook the rice, drain, and rinse well. Chop two of the eggs and slice the other for decoration. Melt the butter in a saucepan then add the cooked rice, the flaked fish, and the chopped eggs. Season with salt and cayenne pepper and heat through, stirring all the time until piping hot. Serve garnished with chopped parsley and slices of hard-boiled egg.

MEAT

Boiled Leg of Mutton

*1 small leg of mutton or
    middle neck of mutton
1½ level tsps salt
water*

*4 carrots, halved if large
2 sticks of celery,
    chopped
1 small turnip, chopped*

Weigh the meat and allow 25 minutes per pound, plus 25 minutes. Place the wiped meat in a saucepan with salt and water to cover. Bring to the boil and skim if necessary. Add the carrots, celery, and turnip to the mutton. Simmer slowly until the meat is tender. Then drain and serve with onion sauce (see below).

Onion Sauce

2 onions, chopped
1 oz butter
1 oz flour
milk
salt and pepper

Simmer the onions in salted water until soft. Drain well and keep the water. Melt the butter over a low heat, then stir in the flour and cook slowly without browning for 2 or 3 minutes. Remove from heat and gradually blend in the water from the onions and enough milk to make up to ½ pint. Return to heat and stir constantly until sauce thickens. Stir in the cooked onion and season to taste.

Cumberland Mutton Pies

1-lb piece of leg of
* mutton, or fillet of loin*
* of mutton, or boned*
* shoulder of mutton*
1 bay-leaf
salt and pepper
1 large onion, chopped
1 carrot, diced
8 oz well-chilled short-
* crust pastry (see below)*
beaten egg or milk

Cut the meat into small cubes and stew gently with the onion, carrot, bay-leaf, and seasoning in the minimum amount of water until cooked — about 1 hour. Leave until cold. Roll out half the pastry and cut it into rounds to fill eight to ten large patty tins. Fill them with the meat and vegetable mixture and a little of the stock which it was cooked in. Roll out the remaining pastry, cut it into rounds, dampen, and place over the filling. Cut a slit in the top of each. Brush with beaten egg or milk to glaze and bake at 400°F for about 30 minutes.

Shortcrust Pastry

8 oz plain flour
a pinch of salt
2 oz lard

2 oz margarine
water

Sift the flour and salt together. Cut the fat into pieces, then rub it into the flour, using fingertips only, until it resembles fine breadcrumbs. Using a round-ended knife, mix in sufficient water to make the mixture begin to stick together. Then, with one hand, knead it together to form a smooth dough. Use it straightaway, or leave it rest for 15 minutes in the refrigerator.

Lancashire Hotpot

8 neck or chump chops
8 oz sliced onions
3 lambs' kidneys
(optional)
1 lb sliced potatoes

salt and pepper
½ pt stock or water
1 oz dripping or lard

Remove the fat from the chops and place them in a greased casserole. Add the onions. Skin and dice the kidneys and add, then add the potatoes. Season the ingredients well with salt and pepper. Finally, pour in the stock or water (stock-cubes may be used). Brush the potatoes with melted dripping or lard. Put the lid on the casserole and cook in the middle of the oven at 325°F for 2½ hours, or until the meat and potatoes are tender.

Irish Stew

8 neck or chump chops   *salt and pepper*
2 large onions, sliced   *chopped parsley*
2 lb potatoes, sliced

Trim fat from the chops. Place alternate layers of meat and vegetables in a greased casserole, finishing with a layer of potatoes; season. Add enough water to half-cover the ingredients. Place lid on casserole and cook in the middle of the oven at 375°F for 2 hours, when the top layer of potatoes should begin to brown. Sprinkle the stew with chopped parsley before serving.

Tripe and Onions

1½ lb tripe   *salt and pepper*
3 medium onions, sliced   *1 oz flour*
½ pt water
½ pt milk

Blanch the tripe and cut into 3-inch squares. Place in a saucepan with water, milk, and salt and pepper. Bring to the boil, add the onions, then simmer gently for 2 hours. Mix the flour to a paste with some milk then place in the saucepan to thicken the sauce. Stir until boiling, then simmer for 20 minutes.

Roast Beef

a joint of beef suitable for roasting — sirloin, topside, etc.

Wipe and weigh the meat and work out the cooking time. Allow 20 minutes per pound plus 20 minutes if the meat is rolled or on the bone, at 425°F. A meat thermometer can be very useful, as are oven bags, but this is a matter of preference. Follow the manufacturer's instructions. Place the joint in a baking tin in the middle of the oven with the fat at the top of the joint. Beef is best served slightly rare with the traditional accompaniments, such as Yorkshire pudding (see below), horseradish cream (see below), gravy, and vegetables.

Yorkshire Pudding

4 oz plain flour
a pinch of salt
1 or 2 eggs

½ pt milk
1 oz lard or dripping

Sieve the flour and salt together. Make a well in the centre and break in the egg (two eggs make the mixture much lighter). Add half the milk and gradually mix in the flour, drawing it in from the sides of the bowl. Add the remaining milk gradually and beat well until the ingredients are thoroughly mixed. (Alternatively, all the ingredients may be put into a liquidizer until thoroughly blended). Heat the lard or dripping in a baking tin in a moderately hot oven (400°F) until smoking. Then pour in the batter. Bake until the pudding is risen and brown — 20 to 30 minutes.

Horseradish Cream

2 tbsps grated horse-
radish
2 tbsps lemon juice
2 tsps sugar

a pinch of mustard
¼ pt thickened cream
whipped

Combine the horseradish, lemon juice, sugar, and mustard, then add the whipped cream.

Shepherd's Pie

8 oz minced left-over
   roast beef
1 lb potatoes
1 oz butter
2 tbsps milk
salt and pepper

1 medium onion,
   chopped
dripping or oil
1 tbsp chopped parsley
stock or left-over gravy

Boil and drain the potatoes, then mash them with the butter, milk, and salt and pepper. Fry the onion in some dripping or oil. Mix together the meat, onion, parsley, and stock or gravy to moisten. Put this mixture into a greased ovenproof dish or casserole, and cover with the mashed potatoes. Press down well, using a fork to make a pattern. Bake for 30 minutes in the middle of a moderate oven (375°F).

Sea Pie

1½ lb stewing steak
seasoned flour
1 large or 2 small onions,
   diced
1 carrot, diced

1 small turnip, diced
stock or water
12 oz suet crust pastry
   (see page 21)

Remove all fat and gristle from the steak and cut into cubes. Coat the meat with seasoned flour. Place the vegetables and meat in a saucepan, cover with stock or water, then bring to the boil. Cover and simmer gently for 1½ hours. Roll out the suet crust pastry into a round to fit inside the saucepan. Cook for an additional hour until suet is well risen.

Suet Crust Pastry

4 oz suet
8 oz self-raising flour

½ tsp salt
cold water

Mix together the flour, suet, salt, and enough water to make a light dough. Knead lightly.

Beefsteak Pie

1½ lb stewing steak
seasoned flour
2 onions, chopped
stock or water and
* stock-cubes*

8 oz flaky pastry (see
* page 48) or shortcrust*
* pastry (see page 17)*
beaten egg or milk

Wipe the meat thoroughly and remove all fat, skin, and gristle carefully. Cut meat into small cubes and dip in the seasoned flour. Place the meat in a greased pie-dish together with the onions. Add enough stock to three-quarters cover the meat. Place a pie funnel in the centre of the dish. Roll out the pastry to ½-inch thickness, and as big as the pie-dish, plus 1 inch. Cut a ¾-inch strip from round the edge of the pastry to cover the rim of the pie-dish. Brush the rim of the pie-dish with water and place the strip of pastry round it. Dampen and seal the join. Dampen the pastry lid and place over the dampened strip. Press the edges firmly together. Make a hole in the centre of the pie to allow the steam to escape. Decorate the top of the pie with pastry leaves. Glaze with beaten egg or milk. Bake in the middle of a very hot oven (450°F) for 15 minutes. Reduce the heat to 375°F and cook for a further 1¾ hours. If the pastry becomes too brown, cover it with greaseproof paper.

Dad's Favourite Steak and Kidney Pudding

12 oz stewing steak
4 oz kidneys
suet crust pastry (see
 page 21)
seasoned flour
1 large onion, chopped
water

Reserve one-quarter of the pastry for a lid. Roll out the remainder to ¼-inch thickness and line a greased 1½-pint pudding basin with it. Remove all skin and gristle from the steak and cut it into ¼-inch cubes. Remove the skin and core from kidneys and cut them into slices. Coat the meat and kidneys with seasoned flour. Fill the lined basin with the meat, kidneys, and onion together with 3 tablespoons of water. Roll out the remaining pastry for the lid, brush with water, and place it on top of the meat, sealing the pastry edges well. If you are using an aluminium basin, grease the lid and place firmly on; *or* cover with greased greaseproof paper and a cloth tied round with string. Steam the pudding over boiling water for about 4 hours; if the meat is stewed first, this time may be reduced to 2 to 2½ hours.

Cornish Pasties

12 oz good stewing steak
12 oz shortcrust pastry
 (see page 17)
2 medium potatoes, diced
1 onion, diced
salt and pepper

Remove all the fat from the steak and cut into small cubes. Divide the pastry into four equal portions and roll out into rounds about the size of a saucer. Divide the meat and vegetables into four equal portions and place each portion on a round of pastry; season. Wet the edges then press together, so that the join is at the top of the pasty, then flute the edges with your fingers. Bake the pasties in a hot oven (425°F) for 15 minutes, then at 325°F for 45 minutes, until the pastry is golden brown and the meat and vegetables are cooked. Cornish pasties may be eaten hot or cold.

Potted Beef and Ham

1 lb shin beef
8 oz lean ham
1 egg
¼ pt cold water

3-4 oz soft breadcrumbs
grated nutmeg
salt and pepper

Mince the beef and ham together and mix well. Beat the egg and add it to the beef and ham, together with the water, breadcrumbs, nutmeg, and seasoning. Place the mixture in a greased basin, cover it with greased greaseproof paper, then foil. Secure the foil with string round the rim. Steam for 3 hours, replenishing the water when needed.

Toad in the Hole

Yorkshire pudding batter   1 lb sausages
* (see page 19)*

Place the uncooked sausages in a rectangular dish or baking tin. Beat the batter and pour in round the sausages. Bake in a moderately hot oven (400°F) for 20 to 30 minutes until the batter is well risen, and the sausages nicely browned.

Cold Tongue

Tongue may be eaten with salads, as an accompaniment to ham, and also as a breakfast dish.

1 pickled ox-tongue   *1 carrot, peeled*
1 onion, peeled   *a bunch of mixed herbs*

Weigh the tongue, then wash it and soak for about 2 hours. Place in a pan of cold water together with the onion, carrot, and herbs. Bring to the boil, then simmer gently for 30 minutes per pound, plus 20 minutes. Remove the skin from the tongue carefully and place the tongue in a bowl. Curl it round tightly. Place a saucer with a weight on top, and leave it until the tongue is cold.

Baked Chops with Pineapple

4 pork chops   *salt and pepper*
8-oz tin pineapple rings   *brown sugar*

Remove skin and excess fat from chops, place in an ovenproof dish, and add salt and pepper. Add enough pineapple juice to come half-way up the chops. Cover them with foil and cook in the middle of a moderate oven until tender — about 45 minutes. Remove foil, garnish each chop with a pineapple ring, sprinkle them with brown sugar, and return to oven for 5 to 10 minutes, until the sugar has just melted.

Pork Pie

*1½ lb lean loin, leg, or
   shoulder of pork*
salt and pepper
¾ pt pork or chicken stock

*hot-water crust pastry
   (see below)*
beaten egg

Cut the meat into small cubes and season with salt and
pepper. Place in a saucepan with the stock and simmer
until tender — about 1 hour. Boil or reduce the stock
until it measures ½ pint. Cool the meat and stock. Make
the pastry, then roll out and shape over a jam-jar or tin
about 4 inches in diameter, using your hands or a pie
mould. Place the cold cooked meat in the pastry case,
add some stock, and use the remaining quarter of the
pastry to make a lid and trimmings. Three or four folds
of greased greaseproof paper should be placed round
the pie to preserve its shape and stop it from becoming
too brown. Make a hole in the centre of the pie.
Decorate the pie with pastry leaves. Glaze with beaten
egg. Bake in a hot oven (425°F), then lower the heat to
350°F when the pastry is set — about 15 minutes. Bake
for about 1½ hours. Brush the sides with beaten egg.
When the pie is baked and still hot, reheat the
remainder of the stock and pour into the pie, using a
funnel poked through the hole in the centre of the pie
top.

Hot-Water Crust Pastry

8 oz plain flour
1 level tsp salt
3 oz lard
½ pt water or milk

¼ tsp pepper

Sift the flour and salt into a mixing bowl; make a well in the centre. Heat the lard in a saucepan with the water and seasoning until boiling-point is reached. Pour the hot liquid into the well in the flour and mix in with a knife. Knead until smooth and use while still warm.

Grandma Perry's Faggots

These faggots may be eaten hot with vegetables, cold and sliced, reheated wrapped in foil, or fried and served with bacon for a delicious breakfast or supper dish.

*1 lb pig's liver or fry (or
  a pig's pluck as it is
  known in the butcher-
  ing industry)
3 medium onions
6 oz fat pork
a pinch of basil and
  thyme
1 level tsp powdered sage
½ tsp grated nutmeg*

*salt and pepper
2 medium eggs
fresh breadcrumbs*

Thinly slice the liver, onions, and pork. Place in a saucepan with the basil, thyme, sage, nutmeg, and salt and pepper. Just cover with water and simmer for half an hour. Strain off the liquid and save it for gravy if required. Mince finely, and add the beaten egg and enough breadcrumbs to make a fairly firm mixture. Press into a well-greased baking tin and mark into squares. Bake in the middle of a moderately hot oven (400°F) until lightly browned. Thicken the stock for gravy, if serving with vegetables.

Bacon in Cider

6-lb cut of bacon
1 pt cider
a bunch of sweet herbs
1 cup brown bread-
  crumbs

2 oz brown sugar
12 cloves

Weigh bacon and soak overnight in a pan of water. Bring to the boil next day, then pour off the water and bring to the boil again in fresh water. Add the herbs and simmer slowly, allowing 20 minutes to the pound, and adding the cider 1½ hours before the meat is done. After cooking, cool the bacon and skin it. Cover with breadcrumbs and sugar and stick in the cloves. Bake in a moderate oven (350°F) until brown.

Yorkshire Rabbit

This recipe comes from Nidderdale in the Yorkshire Dales.

1 rabbit
salt and pepper
vinegar
2 oz butter
8 oz chopped onions

4 cloves
mixed herbs
¼ pt water
flour
1 tsp sugar

Wash and cut up the rabbit (skinned) and place in a bowl. Sprinkle with salt and pepper and cover with vinegar. Stand overnight. Melt butter in a pan and put in the rabbit, the onion, cloves, a sprinkling of herbs, the water, and the vinegar in which the rabbit was soaked. Let the pan simmer for 1½ hours, stirring occasionally. Thicken with flour before serving and add the sugar.

Gipsy Pie

1 young rabbit	*stock*
8 oz cooked ham	*flaky pastry (see page 48)*
8 oz stewing steak	*or*
nutmeg	*shortcrust pastry (see*
4 tsps chopped parsley	*page 17)*
salt and pepper	*beaten egg or milk*

Joint the rabbit and soak it in cold, salted water for 2 hours. Slice the ham. Prepare the steak by cutting off all fat and gristle; then cut into cubes. Place the rabbit, ham, and steak in a greased pie-dish. Sprinkle with the nutmeg and parsley, and add pepper and salt to taste. Add enough stock to come half-way up the dish, or almost cover the meat, and cover with pastry. Glaze with beaten egg or milk. Bake the pie slowly in a moderate oven (375°F) for 2 hours. Cover the top with greased greaseproof paper if the pastry turns too brown.

Roast Pheasant

1 pheasant	*butter*
8 oz bacon	*flour*

The pheasant should be 'well hung', like all game, that is for ten to eleven days, or even longer if the weather is frosty. Otherwise, the flesh will be tasteless and dry. Pluck, draw, and truss the pheasant. Cover the breast with strips of bacon, preferably fatty. Roast in the

middle of the oven at 450°F for 10 minutes, then lower
the heat to 400°F, and cook the bird for a further 30 to 40
minutes, according to its size. Baste often with butter.
Fifteen minutes before the cooking is completed, take
away the bacon, dredge the breast of the pheasant with
flour, baste well and continue cooking. Take away the
trussing strings and place the bird on a hot dish.
Garnish with watercress. Serve with thin gravy, game
chips, fried crumbs, and bread sauce. A light tossed
salad goes well with roast pheasant.

PUDDINGS

Rhubarb Fool

1 lb rhubarb
4 oz sugar
nuts

¼ pt custard
¼ pt thickened cream

Stew the fruit in a small amount of water, adding the sugar to taste. Chop the nuts. Sieve the fruit, then fold it into the custard, then fold in the cream. Pour into individual glasses and decorate with the nuts. Serve with sponge fingers or shortbread. This dessert may also be made with raspberries, blackberries, apricots, or gooseberries.

Brandy Syllabub

grated rind and juice of 1
  lemon
2 tbsps sherry
2 tbsps brandy

3 oz castor sugar
½ pt thickened cream

Marinate the lemon rind with the juice for 2 hours. Combine this with the sherry, brandy, and sugar and lastly the whipped cream. Serve with sponge fingers or macaroon biscuits.

Sherry Trifle

3 sherry glasses sherry
8-oz tin fruit
8 individual sponge
  cakes (small)
jam
1 packet jelly crystals
  dissolved in 1 pt water
12 small macaroons
1 pt custard

½ pt thick cream
sugar
glacé cherries, angelica,
  nuts, etc.

Strain the juice from the fruit. Halve the sponge cakes and spread them with plenty of jam. Arrange them in a dish and pour the sherry and fruit juice over them. Scatter over the fruit, pour on the jelly, and leave to set. Crush the macaroons and sprinkle over the top. Make the custard, allow it to cool, and pour it over the top. Whip the cream and sweeten to taste. Spread the cream over the custard, keeping some to pipe round as a decoration. Decorate the trifle with nuts, angelica, cherries, etc.

Caramel Custard

4 oz sugar	*1 pt milk*
¼ pt water	*4 eggs*

Put the sugar and water in a saucepan and heat until the sugar dissolves. Bring to the boil, but do not stir until it caramelises: that is, when it turns a rich brown colour. Pour the mixture into a warmed 6-inch cake tin. Turn the tin until the bottom is completely covered by the caramel. Set aside to cool. Warm the milk, then add the beaten eggs and strain over the caramel. Put the tin in a *bain-marie*, or a baking tin with about 1 inch of cold water, and bake in the middle of the oven at 350°F until set — about 40 minutes. Turn out and serve at once. This pudding may be served cold by letting it cool, and then chilling it completely in the refrigerator.

Summer Pudding

6 oz sugar	*6 oz thinly sliced white*
3 tbsps water	*bread*
1 lb raspberries or	*whipped cream*
blackberries	

Dissolve the sugar in the water and slowly bring it to the boil; add the fruit and simmer gently until it is soft. Remove the crusts from the bread. Line a 1½-pint pudding basin with slices of bread. Pour in the fruit and make a lid with the rest of the bread. Place a saucer on top of the pudding and keep it pressed down with a weight (an unopened tin will suffice). Leave the pudding overnight, or for 12 hours in the refrigerator. Turn it out on to a deep plate. Serve with cream.

Bread and Butter Pudding

3-4 slices of bread and   *¾ pt milk*
   butter   *2 eggs*
2 oz currants or sultanas   *ground nutmeg*
½ oz castor sugar

Cut the bread and butter into slices and place, buttered side up, in layers in a greased ovenproof dish together with the fruit and sugar. Warm the milk almost to boiling-point. Whisk the eggs lightly then pour the warmed milk on to them, stirring at the same time; strain the mixture over the bread. Sprinkle the top of the pudding with ground nutmeg and bake in the middle of the oven at 350°F for 30 to 40 minutes, until set and lightly browned.

Bread Pudding

8 oz white bread   *2 oz sugar*
  (preferably stale)   *2 level tsps mixed spice*
½ pt milk   *1 large egg*
4 oz sultanas or currants   *nutmeg*
2 oz raisins or candied   *castor sugar*
  peel
2 oz beef suet

Grease a 1½-pint pie-dish. Break up the bread and pour the milk on it. Allow to soak for half an hour, then beat well. Add the sultanas and raisins. Grate the suet and add, together with the sugar and spice. Combine thoroughly. Add the beaten egg and more milk if necessary until the mixture is of a dropping consistency. Pour into the pie-dish. Sprinkle with powdered or freshly grated nutmeg. Bake in the middle of the oven at 350°F for 1½ to 2 hours. Sprinkle the pudding with castor sugar before serving.

Queen of Puddings

¾ pt milk
grated rind of 1 lemon
1 oz butter
2 eggs, separated
2 oz castor sugar

3 oz fresh white bread-
   crumbs
2 tbsps raspberry or
   strawberry jam

Warm the milk with the lemon rind and butter. Whisk the egg-yolks with 1 ounce of the castor sugar, then pour on the milk, stirring thoroughly. Strain over the breadcrumbs and pour into a 2-pint ovenproof dish; leave to soak for 10 minutes. Bake at 350°F for 25 minutes. Remove from the oven and spread the top with the warmed jam. Whisk the egg-whites until stiff, then add the rest of the sugar, and beat in thoroughly. Place this on top of the jam and bake for a further 20 minutes until the meringue is slightly browned.

Rice Pudding

1½ oz short-grain rice
1 oz sugar
1 pt milk
1 dsp butter

ground nutmeg

Place the rice and sugar in a greased ovenproof dish. Pour on the milk, top with shavings of butter, and sprinkle nutmeg on the top. Bake in the middle of the oven for 2 hours at 300°F.

Apple Fritters

Batter

4 oz plain flour
a pinch of salt
1 egg

¼ pt milk or milk and water

Fritters

4 cooking apples
fat

castor sugar
cinnamon

Batter: Make a well in the middle of the flour and salt and break in the egg. Add half the liquid and beat until smooth. Gradually add the remainder of the liquid and beat until well mixed.

Fritters: Peel and core the apples. Cut them into rings ¼ inch thick. Dip them in the coating batter and fry them until golden brown in some deep fat which is hot enough to brown a piece of bread in 60 to 70 seconds. Drain the fritters on crumpled kitchen paper, add castor sugar and cinnamon, and serve at once.

Variations

Pineapple Fritters: Use drained tinned pineapple rings.

Banana Fritters: Use small bananas, peeled and cut into lengths.

Baked Apples

6 even-sized cooking apples
soft brown sugar

dates, raisins, sultanas, or other dried fruit
6 tbsps water

Wipe the apples and core them carefully. Make a slit

round the skin at the middle of each apple to prevent them from bursting as they cook. Place the apples in a lightly buttered ovenproof dish and stuff the core holes with sugar and dried fruits. Pour water round the apples in the dish and bake at 350° to 400°F for about 45 minutes until the apples are soft and look fluffy. Serve hot with custard or cream.

Apple Dumplings

4 medium cooking apples, peeled and cored
8 oz shortcrust pastry (see page 17)

3 oz sugar
milk or beaten egg
castor sugar

Divide the pastry into four pieces and roll out each one to about 9 inches in diameter. Place an apple on each round of pastry and fill up the core holes with the sugar. Brush all edges of the pastry with water, then bring them to the top and press them together to form a seal. Place the dumplings, sealed edge down, on a greased oven tray. Use any remains of the pastry to make pastry leaves and trim the tops of the dumplings. Brush the tops thoroughly with beaten egg or milk to glaze. Bake in the middle of the oven at 425°F for 15 minutes, then at 325°F for about 20 minutes, until the apples are soft and the pastry nicely browned. Sprinkle with castor sugar before serving.

Bakewell Tart

4 oz shortcrust pastry (see page 17)

2 oz cake crumbs
2 oz ground almonds

raspberry jam
2 oz butter
2 oz sugar
1 egg

almond essence
icing sugar

Roll out the pastry to line a pie-plate or flan ring. Spread this well with raspberry jam. Cream the butter and sugar together until pale and fluffy. Beat in the egg and then mix in the cake crumbs, ground almonds, and a few drops of almond essence. Spread the mixture evenly on top of the jam and bake in a hot oven (about 400°F) for half an hour. Sprinkle with sieved icing sugar, and serve either hot or cold.

Shropshire Mincemeat

A traditional English mincemeat for mince pies.

1 lb suet
2 lb finely chopped
  apples
2 lb currants
1½ lb raisins, seeded and
  chopped
1½ lb castor sugar
8 oz finely shredded
  mixed candied peel
grated rind and juice of 4
  lemons

1 tsp cinnamon, 1 tsp
  ground mace, and 1 tsp
  nutmeg mixed
  together
2 cups brandy

Mix all the ingredients together well, press into a jar, and cover closely. Store the mincemeat in a cool dry place until required: it will keep for at least one month.

Brandy Butter

This is traditionally served with Christmas pudding and mince pies.

3 tbsps brandy   3 oz castor sugar
3 oz butter

Cream the butter and sugar until pale and fluffy. Add the brandy drop by drop to prevent the mixture from curdling. Put in a small dish and leave to harden before serving.

Spotted Dick

3 oz suet   6 oz currants
3 oz self-raising flour 2 oz castor sugar
3 oz breadcrumbs   milk

Grate the suet. Mix all the dry ingredients together, then add enough milk to make a fairly soft dough. Form into a roll, wrap up in a well-floured cloth loosely tied with string at the ends, and boil for 1½ hours to 2 hours. Alternatively, add enough milk to make a soft dropping consistency, and then steam the mixture in a greased 1½-pint basin for 2 hours.

Roly-Poly Pudding

12 oz self-raising flour water
a pinch of salt   jam
6 oz suet

Sift the flour and salt together. Grate or finely chop the suet. Add suet to the flour and mix it with water to form a soft dough. Roll out the dough and spread with jam up to ¼ inch from the edges of the dough. Moisten the edges with water and roll up loosely, sealing the edges. Place the pudding in a floured cloth, tying up the ends with string. Lower into fast boiling water, adding more boiling water if necessary to keep the pudding covered, and simmer for 2½ hours.

King George I's Christmas Pudding

Sometimes known as 'the Pudding King', King George enjoyed a Christmas pudding made from this recipe at his first Christmas dinner in England in 1714. It was used at Sandringham many times afterwards.

1½ lb finely shredded suet
1 lb dried plums, stoned
and halved
1 lb mixed peel, cut in
long strips
1 lb small raisins
1 lb sultanas
1 lb currants
1 lb sifted flour
1 lb sugar
1 lb brown crumbs
1 heaped tsp mixed spice
½ nutmeg, grated

2 tsps salt
1 lb eggs, weighed in
their shells
½ pt milk
juice of 1 lemon
1 large wineglass brandy

Mix the dry ingredients and fruit, moisten them with the eggs, which have been beaten to a froth, and the milk, lemon juice, and brandy mixed together. Stand for at least 12 hours in a cool place, then turn into buttered moulds. Boil for 8 hours at first, then for 2 hours before serving. This quantity makes three 3-pound puddings.

CAKES

Cumberland Sand Cake

This cake, a type of Madeira cake, was very popular in Edwardian times.

4 oz butter	grated rind of 1 lemon
5 oz castor sugar	6 oz cornflour
3 eggs	1 level tsp baking powder

Cream the butter and sugar until pale and fluffy. Beat in the eggs one at a time. Add the lemon rind together with the sifted cornflour and baking powder. Place the mixture in an oblong tin 8 by 4 inches and bake in the middle of a moderate oven at 350°F for about 1¼ hours. If you wish, dust the top of the cake when cool with sifted icing sugar.

Victoria Sandwich Cake

6 oz butter or margarine   *6 oz self-raising flour*
6 oz castor sugar   *approx. 3 tbsps jam*
3 large eggs

Grease two sandwich tins and line the bottoms with greased greaseproof paper. Cream the butter and sugar until pale and fluffy. Beat the eggs and add a little at a time, beating well. Fold in the flour gradually. Add a little water if the mixture is at all dry and place half the mixture in each tin, levelling it with a knife. Bake the cakes on the same shelf in the middle of the oven at 375°F for about 20 minutes, when they should be golden brown and firm to the touch. Turn them out to cool and sandwich them together with jam. Dredge the top with castor sugar or sieved icing sugar.

Old English Cider Cake

1 cup cider   *8 oz flour*
4 oz butter   *2 tsps grated nutmeg*
4 oz sugar   *1 tsp bicarbonate of soda*
2 eggs

Cream the butter and sugar until pale and fluffy. Beat in the eggs one at a time. Sift the flour with the nutmeg and bicarbonate of soda and add half of this to the mixture. Beat the cider until frothy and stir in carefully, then add the remaining half of the flour. Bake in a well-greased shallow tin at 450°F for about 45 minutes.

Farmhouse Pound Cake

8 oz butter
8 oz sugar
4 medium eggs
8 oz flour
1 level tsp baking powder
½ tsp salt
2 oz chopped mixed peel
grated rind and juice of 1
*   lemon*
2 oz glacé cherries
8 oz sultanas

Prepare and line an 8-inch cake tin. Cream the butter and sugar together until pale and fluffy, then add the beaten eggs and the rest of the ingredients. Milk may be added to make a soft, dropping consistency. Put the mixture into the tin and bake for 1¾ to 2¼ hours.

Yorkshire Parkin

8 oz plain flour
2 level tsps ground
*   cinnamon*
4 level tsps ground ginger
1 level tsp bicarbonate of
*   soda*
8 oz oatmeal (porridge
*   oats)*
4 oz margarine or lard
4 oz treacle
4 oz golden syrup
4 oz sugar
1 egg
¼ pt milk

Line a 9-inch tin with greased greaseproof paper. Sift together the flour, cinnamon, ginger, bicarbonate of soda, then add the oatmeal, and mix well together. Melt the fat, treacle, syrup, and sugar carefully over a very low heat. Beat the egg. Make a well in the middle of the dry ingredients. Add the warm melted mixture, the beaten egg, and enough milk to give a soft consistency. Pour into the tin and bake near the bottom of the oven at 350°F for about 1 to 1¼ hours.

Grasmere Shortcake

8 oz flour
4 oz moist brown sugar
¼ tsp baking soda
½ tsp ground ginger
4 oz butter

Filling

a small quantity of chopped preserved ginger and 1 tsp of the syrup
2 oz butter
4 oz icing sugar

Line a shallow baking tin with greased paper. Put the dry ingredients in a bowl and rub in the butter until it has the consistency of breadcrumbs. Empty the mixture into the prepared tin. Spread evenly with the hand and press down very lightly. Bake in a very moderate oven until nicely browned. Turn out, cool, then trim the edges and cut in half. Spread the filling evenly on one of the pieces of cake and press the other piece into position on top. This can be kept in an airtight tin until needed.

Filling: Cream the butter and sugar. Add the chopped ginger and syrup.

Gingerbread

1 lb plain flour
1 level tbsp ground ginger
1 level tsp salt
6 oz butter or margarine
8 oz brown sugar

1 level tbsp bicarbonate	6 oz treacle
of soda	6 oz golden syrup
1 level tbsp baking	1 egg
powder	½ pt milk

Grease and line an 8-inch square tin with greased greaseproof paper. Sift the flour, ginger, bicarbonate of soda, baking powder, and salt together. Carefully warm, but do not boil, the butter, sugar, treacle, and syrup. Mix in the beaten egg and the milk. Make a well in the centre of the dry ingredients. Pour in the melted mixture and mix carefully and thoroughly together. Place the mixture in the prepared tin and bake in the middle of the oven at 325°F until firm to the touch — about 1½ hours.

Simnel Cake

6 oz butter or margarine	8 oz flour
8 oz castor sugar	2 oz shredded candied
8 oz eggs, weighed in	peel
their shells	6 oz currants

Almond Paste

| 3 oz ground almonds | 1 small egg |
| 6 oz castor sugar | |

Cream the butter and sugar. Add each egg separately and stir in the flour, candied peel, and currants as lightly as possible. Place half the cake mixture in a lined cake tin, add the almond paste, and top with the rest of the cake mixture. Bake in a moderate oven for 45 minutes to 1 hour.

Almond Paste: Mix the ground almonds, sugar, and

egg to a stiff paste and roll out to the size of the cake tin.

Olive's Tipsy Cake

1 ginger cake
whisky
¾ pt cream, whipped
12 cherries

Place the ginger cake on a flat dish and cut it lengthwise into three layers. Remove the upper layers. Fill a tablespoon with whisky and sprinkle it on to the bottom layer of ginger cake (do not let it become too wet). Spread a layer of cream on top, then place the middle layer of cake on this. Sprinkle more whisky over the cake. Spread on another layer of cream, then put the last layer of cake on top. Sprinkle over more whisky. Spread cream over the top and sides of the cake. Cut the cherries in half and decorate the cake with them. Place in a cool spot until required.

Fat Rascals, or Turf Cakes

On the Whitby moors, Yorkshire, these were called Turf Cakes, as they were cooked on a griddle over a peat or turf fire.

8 oz self-raising flour
4 oz lard
3 oz sugar
1 oz currants
1 oz sultanas
a pinch of salt
1 egg

Rub the lard into the flour until the mixture resembles fine breadcrumbs. Add sugar, currants, sultanas, and salt and mix to a fairly soft dough with the beaten egg. Roll out the dough to ½-inch thickness and cut into

rounds. Bake in a hot oven (425°F) until brown —
about 15 minutes.

Queen Cakes

4 oz butter or margarine *4 oz self-raising flour*
4 oz castor sugar *2 oz sultanas*
2 eggs *milk*

Cream the butter and sugar until pale and fluffy. Beat
the eggs together and add, a little at a time, to the butter
and sugar, beating well. Mix the flour and fruit
together and carefully fold into the mixture. Add a little
milk or water to give a soft consistency. Bake in twelve
to eighteen patty pans towards the top of the oven at
375°F until well risen and golden brown.

Eccles Cakes

flaky pastry (see below) *½ level tsp nutmeg*
*   or frozen flaky pastry* *milk*
½ oz margarine or butter *sugar*
5 oz currants
4 oz brown sugar
½ level tsp cinnamon

Roll the pastry out thinly and cut into rounds using a 4-
inch cutter. Melt the margarine and mix with the
currants, sugar, cinnamon, and nutmeg. Place a heaped
teaspoon of this mixture in the middle of each round
of pastry. Brush the edges with water and press them
together to form a ball. Turn this over and roll until
the fruit begins to show through. Make the traditional
three cuts on top with a knife. Brush with milk and

sprinkle with sugar. Bake at 450°F on a greased tray until golden brown — about 20 minutes.

Flaky Pastry

8 oz plain flour
a pinch of salt
6 oz butter and lard
  mixed

8 tbsps water

Sift together the flour and salt. Mix and soften the fat with a knife on a plate or marble slab. Divide this equally into four. Rub one-quarter of the fat into the flour until it resembles fine breadcrumbs; mix this to a soft dough with the water. Roll the pastry into an oblong, three times longer than its width, and about ¼ inch thick. Place another quarter of the fat on the top two-thirds of the pastry, in flakes, using a knife. Fold the bottom third up and the top third down. Half turn it round so that the folds are now at the side and seal the edges by pressing with a rolling pin. Roll out carefully again and repeat until all the fat has been used up. Rest the pastry in the refrigerator for at least 45 minutes. It is then easier to use.

Banbury Puffs

2 oz butter or margarine
1 oz stale cake crumbs or
  plain flour
1 egg, separated
2 level tbsps black treacle
4 oz currants, washed and
  dried

1 oz mixed chopped peel
½ level tsp mixed spice
sugar
8oz flaky pastry (see above)
  or rough puff pastry

Melt the butter in a pan, then add the cake crumbs or flour. Cook gently for 3 minutes, stirring. Remove from the heat and beat in the egg-yolk and treacle. Cool the mixture then add the other ingredients. Roll out pastry thinly and cut it into about twelve rounds with a 4-inch plain cutter. Divide the filling mixture equally between the rounds. Moisten the edges of the pastry with water, then draw them together so that the filling is completely covered. Turn each round over, with the join underneath, on to a lightly floured board and press with a rolling pin into an oval shape. Transfer to oven trays. Score the tops into a diamond pattern, or make three diagonal slits on the top of each one. Brush with beaten egg-white and dust lightly with sugar. Leave the puffs in a cool place for 10 minutes. Then bake them in a hot oven (425°F) for 15 to 20 minutes. Cool on a wire tray.

Derek's Brandy Snaps

4 oz butter
7 oz sugar
4 oz golden syrup
4 oz plain flour
1 tsp ground ginger

2 tsps brandy
cream

Melt together in a saucepan the butter, sugar, and syrup. Sift together the flour and ginger and add to them the melted ingredients and the brandy. Place the mixture in teaspoonfuls 6 inches apart on a greased oven tray. Bake for about 10 minutes at 350°F until golden brown. Loosen them with a knife and roll quickly round the greased handle of a wooden spoon. If they are kept warm, they will not break while being rolled. For serving, fill the brandy snaps with whipped cream.

Shrewsbury Biscuits

4 oz butter or margarine   *8 oz plain flour*
4 oz castor sugar   *2 tsps lemon rind*
1 egg

Cream the butter and sugar until pale and fluffy. Add the egg and beat the mixture thoroughly into the flour and lemon rind to make a fairly stiff dough. If the dough is soft, rest it in the refrigerator for 10 to 15 minutes. Knead the dough and roll it out to ¼-inch thickness. Cut into biscuits with a 2½-inch cutter. Bake the biscuits in the upper part of the oven at 350°F until lightly browned — about 15 minutes.

BREAD AND SCONES

Oven Bottom or Plank Bread

This was traditionally baked over a clear fire on the plank, or baking iron. A flat round loaf resulted. As 'oven bottom', it was baked towards the bottom of a fire oven.

2 lb plain flour
1 oz lard
1 level tsp salt
1 oz yeast

1 level tsp sugar
1 large cup milk and
*   water*

Warm the flour in a large bowl. Rub the lard into the

flour and add salt. Cream the yeast with the sugar and mix with the tepid milk and water. Make a well in the centre of the flour and pour in the liquid to make a soft dough. Leave to rise in a warm place for 1 hour. Knead lightly then form into a large flat 'cake' 1 to 1¼ inches thick and round in shape. Leave it to rise for 20 minutes. Place on an oven tray and bake for about 40 minutes at 350° to 400°F until the bottom sounds hollow when tapped and the loaf is golden brown. If you want to make plank bread on a girdle, bake it for 20 minutes on each side, turning once and making sure that the girdle is not too hot, so that the bread bakes thoroughly.

Soda Bread

10 oz whole-wheat flour *1 level tsp salt*
½ tsp bicarbonate of soda *½ pt sour milk or*
1 rounded tsp baking *buttermilk*
* powder*

Place all the ingredients in a bowl and mix them, using enough sour milk to make a dough. Knead lightly on a floured board Form into a round shape. Place on a baking tin and bake in the middle of the oven at 400°F for 20 to 30 minutes. Fly bread is made in the same way; but add a handful of currants to the dry mixture.

Irish Oaten Bread

2 cups rolled oats *2½ cups flour*
2 cups buttermilk or sour *1 tsp bicarbonate of soda*
* milk* *1 tsp salt*

Soak the rolled oats in the buttermilk overnight. Sift

the flour, soda, and salt together; mix in the rolled oats. Knead lightly until smooth and add, if necessary, a little extra flour to maintain a stiff dough. Shape into a round, place on a greased oven tray, and bake in a moderately hot oven (400°F) for 30 to 40 minutes until golden brown and the bottom sounds hollow when tapped with the knuckles.

Chelsea Buns

1 tsp sugar
¼ pt milk
¼ oz dried yeast
8 oz plain flour
¼ tsp salt

1 oz lard or margarine
4 oz currants
1-2 oz sugar
milk or egg

Glaze

1 tbsp sugar

1 tbsp milk

Grease an 8-inch sandwich tin. Put the teaspoonful of sugar with the milk and yeast and stir to start the yeast working. Sieve the flour and salt together and rub in the lard. Add the yeast mixture and extra milk if needed to make a fairly soft dough. Knead thoroughly and leave to rise until double in size. Knead lightly and roll into a 10-inch square. Sprinkle with currants and sugar and roll up like a Swiss roll. Cut into seven or eight pieces and arrange, with the cut side uppermost, in the cake-tin. Leave to prove for 20 minutes, when they will rise to the top of the tin and against one another. Brush with milk or egg and bake in a hot oven (425°F) for about 20 minutes. Brush over with glaze as soon as the buns leave the oven.

Glaze: Dissolve the sugar in the milk.

Wiltshire Lardy Cake

1 lb white bread dough   *granulated sugar*
lard   *mixed spice (optional)*

Roll the dough on a floured pastry board. Place dabs of lard about the size of a walnut and 1½ inches apart on the dough. Sprinkle with sugar and spice. Fold into three from the ends and then into three from the sides. Turn to the right and roll out once more. Repeat this process twice, each time putting on dabs of lard. After three foldings and lardings, roll out to the size of a baking tin, and score with a knife. Bake in a moderate oven until cooked (when a skewer inserted in the middle comes out clean). Sultanas or currants may be added with the spice.

Drop Scones

4 oz self-raising flour   *¼ pt milk*
1 oz sugar   *lard*
1 egg, beaten

Combine the flour and the sugar. Make a well in the centre and mix in the egg and enough milk to make a coating batter like thick cream. Heat a girdle until hot and lightly grease with lard. Drop the mixture from the point of a dessertspoon on to the girdle and when bubbles rise to the surface turn the scones with a palette knife and cook on the other side until golden brown. When cooked, place the scones between two tea-towels to retain the steam and thus keep the scones moist. Serve with whipped cream and jam, or buttered when cold.

Oven Scones

8 oz self-raising flour *¼ pt milk*
½ tsp salt *milk or beaten egg*
2 oz butter or margarine

Sieve the flour with the salt and rub in the butter until the mixture looks like breadcrumbs. Make a well in the centre and add enough milk to form a soft dough. Knead lightly on a floured board and roll out until ¾ inch thick. Cut into rounds with a 2-inch cutter dipped into flour. Place the rounds fairly close together on an oven tray and brush with milk or beaten egg to glaze. Bake near the top of a hot oven (450°F) for 8 to 10 minutes, until well risen and brown. Split when cold and serve buttered. In Devon these scones are served warm, topped with jam and clotted cream.

Singing Hinny, or Northumberland Farmhouse Girdle Cake

This is a North Country girdle cake. It gets its name from the fact that it 'sings' (sizzles) as it cooks.

12 oz self-raising flour *1 oz lard*
1 tsp salt *3 oz currants*
2 oz sugar *½ pt milk and cream*
2 oz ground rice *mixed*

Mix together the flour, salt, sugar, and ground rice. Rub in the lard. Stir in the currants. Add the liquid until the mixture forms a soft dough. Roll out until it is ½ inch thick and prick it all over with a fork. Cut it into halves or quarters so that it is easy to turn and bake on a fairly hot girdle until it is golden brown. Singing Hinnies are delicious split, buttered, and eaten hot.

Welsh Cakes

3 oz butter   *3 oz sugar*
8 oz self-raising flour   *1 egg*
3 oz currants   *milk*

Rub the butter into the flour until the mixture resembles fine breadcrumbs. Add the currants and sugar, then the egg. Mix to a stiff dough with milk. Roll it out to about ½-inch thickness and cook on a girdle over medium heat until the cake is brown on both sides — about 10 minutes altogether.

SAVOURY DISHES AND DRINKS

Bubble and Squeak

left-over cooked potatoes   butter
left-over cooked cabbage
salt and pepper

Mash the potatoes, then combine thoroughly with the cabbage and add salt and pepper to taste. Melt butter in a frying pan over medium heat and spread the cabbage and potato in the pan. Press down well with a fork to make a flat cake. Brown the underside well, then turn over and brown the other side. Cut into pieces and serve with fried bacon as a breakfast or supper dish.

Cornish Potato Cakes

8 oz boiled potatoes   *salt and pepper*
½ oz butter   *2 oz flour*

Mash the boiled potatoes while they are hot with the butter and seasoning. Add the flour and mix thoroughly, then roll out thinly on a well-floured board. Prick well and cut into rounds with a large scone cutter and cook on a greased girdle. Cook the cakes for about 3 minutes on each side, then serve them hot.

Grandma Whitelock's Pease Pudding

Pease pudding traditionally accompanies boiled bacon or ham, and in this case the pease pudding is cooked in its cloth in the same saucepan as the joint of bacon or ham. If the pudding is allowed to go cold, it may be fried with bacon and served as a breakfast dish.

1 lb yellow split peas   *2 oz butter*
1 ham bone   *salt and pepper*

Wash the peas thoroughly and discard any discoloured ones. Tie loosely in a cloth and place in a saucepan with the ham bone and enough boiling water to cover. Cook for 2½ hours until the peas feel soft. Lift out the bag of peas, remove peas from bag, and beat thoroughly with the butter; season.

Cottage Cheese

sour milk   *fresh cream*
salt

Place some milk in a warm place and leave until it is

quite thick. Measure the amount and add ½ teaspoonful of salt for each pint. Stir thoroughly and place in a muslin bag. Hang up to drain overnight, then press between two plates for an hour. Work the cheese up with fresh cream and shape into a pat.

Herb Cheese

approx. 1 tbsp fresh herbs
* - parsley, thyme, sage,*
* chives, tarragon, and*
* marjoram*
4 oz grated mature cheese

3 tbsps sherry or port
2 tbsps thick cream
salt and pepper

Mince the herbs and place in a double boiler or bowl in a saucepan of hot water, together with the grated cheese, sherry, cream, and salt and pepper. Pour into small pots and allow to cool thoroughly before serving.

Welsh Rarebit

8 oz grated Cheddar or
* matured cheese*
1 oz butter
1 tsp dry mustard

4 tbsps brown ale
* (optional)*
salt and pepper
hot buttered toast

Gently heat the cheese, butter, mustard, ale, and salt and pepper in a saucepan until the cheese has melted. Pour over the toast and eat it at once!

Pickled Eggs

You often see pickled eggs in jars in fish-and-chip shops in England. They are delicious with salad, or as a buffet dish.

12 hard-boiled eggs
2 pt cider or white
  vinegar
½ oz black peppercorns

½ oz whole ginger
½ oz allspice
bay-leaves and red
  chillies for decoration

Boil vinegar with spices for 15 minutes. Strain and leave to cool. Remove the eggshells carefully. Place eggs in a wide-mouthed jar with a few bay-leaves and red chillies for decoration. Fill the jar with the vinegar, covering the eggs well. These eggs are ready for use after one week. More hard-boiled eggs may be added to replenish.

Pickled Walnuts

green walnuts
1 lb coarse cooking salt

1 gal water

Spiced Vinegar
2 pt vinegar
¼ oz cinnamon stick
¼ oz cloves

¼ oz root of ginger
¼ oz black peppercorns

Test the walnuts to make sure that the shells have not started to form by pricking them with a needle; if the walnuts are suitable the needle will pass right through them. Stir the salt into the water until dissolved; let the walnuts stand in this for a week. Drain the walnuts and place on clean white (butcher's) paper. Stand them in the sun or a well-lighted place until the walnuts turn black; turn them once or twice to make sure they are black all over. Do this carefully, as the stain is difficult to remove from your fingers! Once the walnuts are black all over, cover them with cold spiced vinegar,

allowing at least 1 to 1¼ inches of vinegar above the walnuts. Cover with plastic wrap. The pickled walnuts will be ready to eat after two months and will keep well.
Spiced Vinegar: Heat the vinegar and spices together until simmering. Remove from the heat and allow to stand for 2 hours. Strain through a sieve and discard the spices.

Pickled Nasturtium Seeds

approx. 8 oz nasturtium seeds
½ pt white or cider vinegar
6 peppercorns
2 bay-leaves
½ tsp salt

Pick out any unripe nasturtium seeds. Wash and dry the others, place them on greaseproof paper on a tray, and leave in the sun for three or four days to dry thoroughly. Simmer the vinegar, peppercorns, bay-leaves, and salt together. Put the seeds in jars and cover with the prepared vinegar. Leave to mature for two months.

Rose-Hip Honey

1 lb rose hips
water
12 oz cooking apples
sugar

Cover the hips with water and boil until tender. Strain through a jelly bag and leave overnight. Cook the apples to a pulp in a small amount of water. Add this to the juice from the hips, then measure it. Allow 1 pound of sugar to each pint of juice. Return the mixture to the pan and cook until it jells when tested. Place in sterilised jars and cover in the normal way.

Lemon Curd

4 eggs, beaten   1 lb sugar
4 oz butter
grated rind and juice of
    4 lemons

Place all the ingredients in a bowl over a saucepan of simmering water or a double boiler. Stir until the sugar has dissolved and the mixture thickens. Strain into sterilised jars and cover and label as for jam. This curd keeps for only about a month, so make it in small quantities only.

Treacle Posset

2 tbsps treacle   juice of 1 large lemon
1 pt milk

Place milk in a saucepan and bring almost to the boil. Add lemon juice and treacle and boil gently until the curd separates. Strain and serve piping hot as a cure for a cold.

Mulled Ale

2 pt ale   3 eggs
8 oz castor sugar   4 oz brandy
1 tsp ground nutmeg   4 oz rum
1 tsp ground ginger

Bring the ale to the boil in a saucepan. Add the sugar,

nutmeg, and ginger. Whip the eggs until they are frothy. Warm the brandy and rum in a small saucepan, pour into the ale mixture, and combine with the eggs. Pour the whole mixture back and forth until it is smooth and creamy. Serve at once.